LOG JAM

on the Sangamon

written, crafted, and photographed by
Caity Peterson & Ellen Saathoff

Dedicated to our children:
Violet, George, Mae, Richie, & Freddy

Down the Sangamon River, in muddy flood plains
where erosion disrupted the local terrains,

while resisting the dragging as water grew high,
stood an Oak tall and true in the summery sky.

And it's broad leafy limbs made a marvelous home
for most all types of creatures - a diverse biome.

When the mighty wind blew, one small Oak branch broke free crashing down to the river through the canopy.

As it bobbed by the bank, this new floating driftwood,
became stuck at the bend, getting landlocked for good.

Soon the current delivered a grand stick collection
with trees of all kinds adding to the selection.

Some crooked and stubby and clunky and stickery,
some Sycamore, Maple, some Oak and some Hickory.

Then rocks, silt, and gravel joined in to the pile,
some in a slurry and some single file.

The sediment traveled through riverbed chases
depositing fragments and filling in spaces.

Now the soil enriched with the food for all plants,
the first bluebells tip-toe a delicate dance,

where White Dutchman's Breeches are anchored with pride
and Mayapples line up the green riverside.

The summer brought mussels cloaked under the sand;
the filtering hearts of a healthy wetland.

Some Heelsplitters, Fatmuckets, Plain Pocketbooks, some Threeridges, Pigtoes, and several Fawnsfoots.

As the days grew more cool, Spotted Sunfish arrived
to the shade of the shallows where Zooplankton thrived.

A silent slow snapper basked out in the sun -
a signal to all that the fall had begun.

Through the cold, sparkling slush on a night with a chill
the Mudpuppies crept in with fluttering gills.

In this haven they found a safe spot to lay eggs,
with the warm vegetation and calm cloudy dregs.

When the spring came again, in a tall budding tree
was a siege of blue herons and new rookery.

The male herons gathered the reeds, moss, and sticks for females to build a snug nest for their chicks.

As the seasons passed by, the environment flourished

every thing taking part to keep all others nourished.

When one branch broke free, it started in motion
the process of slowing the channel erosion.

Saving soil from washing away and providing
a home, at the log jam, of habitats uniting.

The nature life cycle restarts on the mound
as an Oak seedling sprouts from deep under the ground.

From a tree to jam to a tree once again
and with our conservation the story extends.